THE COOLEST CHINESE Foods

Joseph Kampff

NEW YORK

Sinolingua
华语教学出版社

BEIJING

Published in 2022 by The Rosen Publishing Group, Inc.
29 East 21st Street, New York, NY 10010

Jointly published in 2022 by Sinolingua Co.,Ltd., Beijing, China, and The Rosen Publishing Group, Inc., New York, New York, United States.

All rights reserved. No part of this book may be reproduced in any form without permission in writing from the publisher, except by a reviewer.

First Edition

Editor: Joseph Kampff
Designer: Rachel Rising

Photo credits: Cover Maggiezhu/Shutterstock.com; cover, pp. 1–48 Sylfida/Shutterstock.com; cover, pp. 1, 3, 4, 6, 10, 14, 18, 22, 26, 30, 34, 38, 42 CkyBe/Shutterstock.com; pp. 4, 6, 10, 14, 18, 22, 26, 30, 34, 38, 42 photosync/Shutterstock.com; p. 5 https://en.wikipedia.org/wiki/File:Carving_up_our_duck.jpg; p. 7 bonchan/Shutterstock.com; p. 8 feiyuezhangjie/Shutterstock.com; p. 11 K321/Shutterstock.com; p. 12 Chzu/Shutterstock.com; p. 15 TYSB/Shutterstock.com; p. 16 Carrie Fereday/Shutterstock.com; p. 19 Yeo Jung Kim/Shutterstock.com; p. 20 norikko/Shutterstock.com; p. 23 Brent Hofacker/Shutterstock.com; p. 24 kungfu01/Shutterstock.com; p. 27 https://en.wikipedia.org/wiki/File:Charsiubaau_Secondary.jpg; p. 28 TMON/Shutterstock.com; p. 31 Narsil/Shutterstock.com; p. 32 Indian Food Images/Shutterstock.com; p. 35 Kia Nakriz/Shutterstock.com; p. 36 anythings/Shutterstock.com; p. 39 peacefoo/Shutterstock.com; p. 40 Adam Melnyk/Shutterstock.com; p. 43 Yank Yidong/Shutterstock.com.

Some of the images in this book illustrate individuals who are models. The depictions do not imply actual situations or events.

Library of Congress Cataloging-in-Publication Data

Names: Kampff, Joseph, author.
Title: The coolest Chinese foods / Joseph Kampff.
Description: New York : Rosen Publishing, [2022] | Series: Crazy cool China | Includes bibliographical references and index.
Identifiers: LCCN 2021050349 (print) | LCCN 2021050350 (ebook) | ISBN 9781499472431 (library binding) | ISBN 9781499472424 (paperback) | ISBN 9781499472448 (ebook)
Subjects: LCSH: Food habits–China–Juvenile literature. | Chinese–Food–Juvenile literature.
Classification: LCC GT2853.C6 K36 2022 (print) | LCC GT2853.C6 (ebook) | DDC 394.1/20951-dc23/eng/20211021
LC record available at https://lccn.loc.gov/2021050349
LC ebook record available at https://lccn.loc.gov/2021050350

Manufactured in the United States of America

CPSIA Compliance Information: Batch #CSRYA23. For further information, contact Rosen Publishing, New York, New York, at 1-800-237-9932.

Contents

A Worldwide Cuisine

China is one of the oldest continuous cultures in the world. It's one of the world's largest countries in terms of land mass. With well over a billion people, it's the most populous country on the planet. And there are over 40 million overseas Chinese spread throughout the world. China is massive in every way. And this includes Chinese **cuisine**, both in China and in the places where Chinese culture has traveled.

There is a huge variety of Chinese foods. One of the reasons for this is the number of ingredients available to Chinese cooks. If it's edible, Chinese cooks have figured out how to make it delicious. The secret to this is balancing the five flavors our tongues taste: bitter, salty, sour, sweet, and **umami**. Chinese cooks build their dishes according to how each ingredient balances with the others. If there's too much acidity, for example, they'll add something sweet.

Chinese food culture is everywhere. It's tempting to see this as a recent phenomenon with, for example, the late 20th and early 21st century explosion in interest in Chinese food in the United States. But this has always been the case. Throughout world history, Chinese cuisine has flourished in China at the same time as it has spread to and influenced other cultures. Today, essential Chinese ingredients (soy sauce, tofu, and five-spice powder), dishes (hot dumplings, Peking duck, and especially hot pot), and cooking tools (wok, cleaver, and chopsticks) are common in restaurant and home kitchens around the world. Chinese food is a worldwide cuisine.

A chef carves Peking duck at the world-famous Beijing restaurant Quanjude.

Rice

It's hard to imagine Chinese food without rice. Rice is such an important **staple food** in China that the Chinese word *fan* means both "meal" and "rice." And the Chinese have farmed rice for a long, long time. Archaeological evidence shows that rice **cultivation** has been practiced in China for around 10,000 years. The Chinese were also the first to perfect the method of growing rice in rice paddies in the Yangtze valley. Today, China is still the world's largest producer of rice. It grows more than 200 million tons of rice a year.

About two-thirds of Chinese territory is mountainous. To solve the problem of growing crops on mountainous terrain, the Chinese have used terraced farming. To create a terraced farm system, farmers cut a series of steps, or terraces, in the side of a mountain or hill. When it rains, the soil is carried into the lower terraces instead of all the way down the slope. The rice terraces in China aren't just useful for agriculture, they're also beautiful tourist destinations.

One of the most famous rice dishes in China is Yangzhou fried rice. There are a couple stories about the origins of fried rice. One says that it began with Emperor Yang of the Sui dynasty (581–618 CE), who brought the dish to Yangzhou. But the origins of fried rice probably have to do with Chinese people not wanting to waste food. Fried rice is an excellent way to reuse day-old rice.

Yangzhou fried rice is one of the most famous fried rice dishes in China.

Believe it or not, the Great Wall of China is held together with sticky rice mortar.

The Great Wall of China was built to stop enemy armies. It was constructed between the 3rd century BCE and the 17th century CE. When it was completed, the Great Wall of China was the largest military structure in the world and stretched over 12,400 miles (20,000 kilometers). The secret to making the Great Wall so strong and long-lasting is that it's held together with mortar made of lime, water, and sticky rice.

The beauty of fried rice is that you can use almost any ingredients. Yangzhou fried rice typically has rice, egg, sea cucumber, chicken, ham, scallops, shrimp, mushrooms, bamboo shoots, and green peas. But if you travel to Yangzhou looking for fried rice with these exact ingredients, you're unlikely to find it. Chinese chefs and home cooks like to make their own versions of fried rice.

Fried rice is popular outside of China as well. The American version of fried rice usually has rice, egg, scallions and other vegetables, soy sauce, and a protein such as pork, shrimp, or chicken. You'd have a hard time finding a Chinese restaurant in the United States that doesn't have fried rice on the menu.

Soybeans

The Chinese love soybeans. They're a crucial ingredient for Chinese cuisine. Soybeans are not only used in the production of essential Chinese ingredients such as soy milk, soy sauce, and tofu, they're also used to feed livestock like pigs and chickens. In 2020, China imported over 100 million tons of soybeans from around the world.

Soy sauce is one of the most important ingredients in Chinese cuisine. Light soy sauce is used for seasoning most Chinese recipes. Dark soy sauce is thicker and sweeter, and has a stronger flavor. In addition to flavoring food, dark soy sauce is used to add color. Soy sauce is made by **fermenting** soybeans with grains and yeast. The tradition of making soy sauce has its roots in China more than 2,000 years ago.

The Chinese have cultivated soybeans for around 3,000 years. Although the Chinese realized early on that soybeans are potentially a good source of protein, the taste and texture of whole soybeans isn't great. Most of the protein in whole soybeans doesn't get digested by humans. The solution, then, is to use whole soybeans to make other products. One of the most important soybean products in Chinese cuisine is tofu.

Soy sauce is one of the most important ingredients in Chinese cuisine.

Mapo tofu is a quintessential Chinese tofu dish that's easy to make at home.

Why would anyone eat a food that many people describe as smelling like a mixture of sour milk and rotting garbage? Answer: It's delicious, once you get over the smell. Stinky tofu is a common street food all over China, and it's especially popular in Hunan province. The legend goes that it was created by accident in China hundreds of years ago when a merchant opened his jar of tofu and found that it had fermented and smelled terrible. He tasted it anyway and realized it was delicious.

The word "tofu" means bean curd. Tofu is made from **coagulated** soy milk and water to make a curd. It's then pressed into solid blocks that range in texture from silken to extra firm. Unless it's been **marinated**, fermented, or flavored in another way, tofu has a very mild flavor. That's why it appears in so many dishes. Tofu takes on the flavor of the other ingredients you cook it with. It's a good way to make tasty and filling food when more flavorful ingredients like pork or chicken are in short supply.

Mapo tofu, a spicy dish from Sichuan province, is one of the most popular Chinese tofu dishes. The words "mapo tofu" can be translated as "pockmarked grandmother's bean curd." Don't let the name scare you, though. Mapo tofu is a delicious dish of tofu in an oily chili sauce with beef.

Sauce, Vinegar, and Oil

In addition to fresh ingredients, Chinese cuisine uses lots of prepared ingredients. Walking through a Chinese grocery store, you might be overwhelmed by the shelves of sauces, vinegars, pastes, and other ingredients. While there are too many to cover here, there are a few that everyone interested in Chinese food should know: hoisin sauce, oyster sauce, white rice vinegar, and toasted sesame oil.

Sichuan food is known for its spiciness. Because the weather of Sichuan is so hot and humid, the people there eat spicy food, which makes them sweat. Sweating helps to keep them cool. The spice of Sichuan food comes from Sichuan peppercorns. Although we call them peppercorns in English, the spice comes from the husks of dried berries. In addition to heat, Sichuan peppercorns cause a tingling, numbing sensation in the mouth. The Chinese term for this combination of heat and numbing is *málà*.

Hoisin sauce is a thick dark sauce made

from fermented soybean paste and other ingredients. It's a sweet and salty sauce usually used in stir fry and for **glazing** meat. In the United States, hoisin is often referred to as Chinese barbecue sauce. The word "hoisin" comes from a Chinese word that means seafood. But it doesn't have any fish in it, and it isn't typically used with seafood dishes. It does have a fishy aroma, though.

Unlike hoisin, oyster sauce is what it sounds like: a sauce made from oysters. Weirdly, though, it doesn't taste or smell fishy. It's a sweet and salty sauce that

Sichuan peppercorns give food a spicy flavor and create a numbing sensation in the mouth.

Chinese cuisine uses a dizzying number of sauces.

Five-spice powder is an essential spice blend used in Chinese cuisine. It isn't always composed of five spices. In fact, five-spice powder in China usually has just four spices—star anise, cinnamon, cloves, and fennel seeds—but it can have more ingredients too. The "five" in five-spice refers to the flavors the blend covers: bitter, salty, sour, sweet, and umami.

gives Chinese food a big hit of flavor. Oyster sauce is made from **caramelized** oyster juices, salt, and sugar. If you're looking to add sweetness, saltiness, and umami to a dish, add oyster sauce.

White rice vinegar is crucial for adding zing to Chinese dishes. It's made by fermenting rice wine until it becomes vinegar. Rice vinegar (or rice wine vinegar) was invented in China, but it's also used in Japanese cooking, where it's an essential ingredient for sushi rice. Acid is a crucial element in any dish's flavor, so rice vinegar is a must for Chinese cooking.

Toasted sesame oil is made by pressing the oil from toasted sesame seeds. Often added at the end of cooking sauces or in salad dressings, toasted sesame oil is a standard ingredient for adding a toasted, nutty flavor to Chinese dishes. It's one of the main ingredients in the popular dish smashed cucumber salad.

Noodles

In Chinese cuisine, noodles go way back. The earliest archaeological example of noodles in China is a 4,000-year-old bowl of noodles found in northwestern China. The written history of the Chinese noodles we know today begins in the Han dynasty, between 25 and 220 CE. The earliest "recipe" for Chinese noodles is for a dough of flour and water that is torn into small squares and added to a soup called *mian pian*. This soup is still eaten in China, and it's easy to find recipes online.

Certain foods closely associated with Chinese cuisine outside of China aren't of Chinese origin. Fortune cookies are a good example. On the other hand, ramen noodles, which are usually thought of as Japanese, originated in China. The ancestor of ramen noodles is a Chinese soup with wheat noodles. The Japanese learned how to make noodles in this way from the Chinese in the 19th century.

At their most basic, noodles are a **cereal food** of flour mixed with water. Wheat and rice noodles are the most common, but noodles can be made of other flours. Cereal foods based on wheat and rice are the main source of energy for Chinese people. The main difference between Chinese noodles and Italian pasta is that Chinese noodles are usually pulled into long strips to symbolize longevity. Italian pasta is often cut into small pieces. And when you order noodles in a Chinese restaurant, the noodles are usually pulled by hand rather than made with a machine. Beyond the basics, though, the variety of Chinese noodles is astounding.

Unlike most Italian pasta, Chinese noodles are usually pulled by hand.

There are thousands of varieties of noodles in China. One of the spiciest Chinese noodle dishes you'll find is dandan noodles from Chengdu. Chengdu is the capital of Sichuan, and Sichuan cuisine is known for its spice, and particularly for its use of mouth-numbing Sichuan peppercorns. Dandan noodles are long, thin noodles usually served with a spicy sauce made of chili oil, minced pork, and preserved vegetables. The name "dandan" comes from the word for the pole used by street vendors to carry the noodles. The pole had a container on each side, one with noodles, the other with the sauce.

Dandan noodles are a traditional noodle dish from Sichuan province, which is known for spicy food.

Dumplings

Just about every culture in the world has some form of dumpling. Italy has ravioli, Poland has pierogi, and India is known for samosas. But China is the king of dumplings. And China has been making them longer than anyone else. Dumplings have existed in China for more than 1,800 years.

For much of world history, food has been scarce. It makes sense that dumplings are so common around the world. They're a good way to make filling food out of small amounts of meat, like pork, beef, or shrimp and vegetables such as cabbage and scallions. The dough is much more plentiful than meat and more filling than vegetables.

The Chinese have used chopsticks for about 5,000 years. When the Chinese began cutting food into small pieces before cooking around 400 BCE, it became unnecessary to use knives at the table. Chopsticks are all you need.

The legend of Chinese dumplings is that they were invented during the Han dynasty (206 BCE–220CE) by the famous physician Zhang Zhongjing. The story is that when visiting his ancestral home during a particularly brutal winter, he saw that the villagers had frostbite on their ears. He cooked them mutton and chilis wrapped in dough that he shaped into "tender ears," or *jiaozi*.

Potstickers are typical *jiaozi* that are fried on one side to give a different texture.

Chopsticks are a convenient way to eat small bites of food.

Dumplings are one of the most important foods for the Chinese New Year's Eve feast. This is because it is believed they bring wealth in the new year. Dumplings are shaped like Chinese *sycee* (ingots of gold or silver used as currency), so the tradition is that the more dumplings you eat on New Year's Eve, the more money you'll make over the next year.

One of the most famous Chinese dumplings is Cantonese shao mai. It's usually stuffed with pork or shrimp, Chinese black mushrooms, scallions, and ginger. It's seasoned with rice wine, soy sauce, and sesame oil, and has an orange **garnish** of carrots or crab roe on top. Shao mai is a quintessential steamed dumpling on the dim sum cart.

Potstickers are another popular dumpling. These are regular *jiaozi*—stuffed with pork, seafood, or vegetables—that are steamed before being fried in oil so they're crispy on one side and soft on the other.

You don't have to eat out or be a chef to enjoy Chinese dumplings. You can find them frozen in grocery stores around the world.

Bao

Bao, or baozi, is a Chinese bun. Bao come in a variety of sizes, and the meat and vegetable filling options are almost endless. Bao can be **savory** or sweet. Bao is a popular street food all over China, and they're also served in dim sum restaurants. Bao can be slightly sweet because of the sugar in the dough. And the secret to their soft and fluffy texture is the steaming of the dough.

Bao isn't just popular in China. People love them all over the world. Chinese bao have taken on many shapes as they travel through the world. One of the most common forms of bao outside of China is sometimes referred to as hirata bao. These are rolled flat, filled with different ingredients, and folded over like sandwiches. This style of bao is especially common in New York City.

There's a legend that bao was invented during the wars of the Three Kingdoms period (220–280 CE) when a traveling army came to a river it needed to cross. In exchange for

allowing the army to cross safely, the people on the other side demanded that the general pay with the heads of fifty of his soldiers. Instead of chopping off his men's heads, the general sent over buns stuffed with meat.

Char siu bao can be either steamed or baked. Baking gives them a beautiful golden crust.

Chinese soup dumplings, or *xiaolongbao*, may be the perfect food. Soup dumplings combine bread, pork, and hot, flavorful soup in a single bite. The mystery is how they get hot soup inside the pleated dumplings. The secret is to use pork bones and skin to make an aspic (this is a thick, **gelatinous** soup) that thins out when the buns are steamed.

One of the most popular bao is char siu bao. Char siu bao originated in the Cantonese region of China. Because so many Chinese restaurants around the world have been opened by Cantonese immigrants, you can find char siu bao all over. Char siu buns are stuffed with BBQ pork and either steamed or baked. The steamed versions are soft, fluffy, and white, while baked char siu buns have a golden crispy crust. Char siu pork is marinated in a sweet and spicy BBQ sauce and roasted. Although some cooks use red food coloring, traditional char siu pork is notable for its bright red color, which comes from a fermented bean paste curd called *nanru*.

Xiaolongbao consist of a rich, hot pork soup inside a steamed dumpling.

Stir Fry

If you've ever seen the kitchen of a Chinese restaurant, you've probably seen a cook standing over a blazing hot stove, quickly cooking vegetables and proteins in a wok. The English term for this is stir fry. Stir fry isn't a particular food. It's a cooking technique that's popular in China and has spread throughout the world.

Along with the Chinese cleaver, the wok is the most essential and iconic of the Chinese cooking tools. Woks are deep pots with round bottoms that use high heat for quick cooking. There's a Cantonese term for the quality the wok gives to food: *wok hei*, which means "breath of the wok." Although you can find woks made out of all sorts of material—cast iron, stainless steel, and so on—the woks you'll find in most Chinese kitchens are made of inexpensive carbon steel.

Stir frying dishes didn't become common until the development of the wok during the Ming dynasty (1368–1644). The round shape of

the wok is crucial to stir frying. It allows meats and vegetables that have been cut into small pieces to cook quickly in a small amount of oil. This technique not only preserves the texture and flavor of ingredients but also saves on cooking fuel.

Because they cook using high heat, woks are perfect for stir frying small pieces of food.

An invention of Chinese people living in the United States, chop suey can be any ingredients mixed into a stir fry.

Although you can find chop suey in many Chinese American restaurants, it's not a dish you'll see much in China. There are many stories about how chop suey came to be. One is that it was invented in New York City in 1896 when a Chinese diplomat asked his chef to prepare a dish that both Americans and Chinese would like. Chop suey probably comes from the Cantonese dish *tsap seui*, which means "leftover remains." So, chop suey is really a dish made by stir frying whatever's left in the fridge.

There's a French term associated with this that is used in professional kitchens around the world: *mis en place*. It literally means "setting in place," but in the cooking world it means having all your ingredients ready. Because stir fry dishes cook so quickly, it's important to have your *mis en place* in order.

Chinese takeout restaurants around the world serve stir fry dishes because they're fast and delicious. While there are all kinds of sauces that can be made for a stir fry dish, one of the most popular in Chinese takeout is brown sauce. Comparing brown sauce to the French **mother sauces**, Martin Yan, a famous Chinese American chef, calls it "the Chinese mother sauce." It's a sauce usually made with soy sauce, wine, stock, sugar, and a thickener like cornstarch. Brown sauce is a crucial ingredient in stir fried dishes like beef and broccoli, General Tso's chicken, and chow mein.

Dim Sum

When you go out for dim sum, you had better be hungry. Dim sum is a feast of small dishes served with tea for breakfast and lunch in Chinese restaurants. Dim sum is the original brunch. You can usually tell you're having dim sum by the carts full of BBQ pork buns, pan-fried leek dumplings, sticky rice in lotus leaf, and egg tarts wheeled around for table-side service. Dim sum dishes can be either sweet or savory.

Dim sum is usually served with either green or jasmine tea. The hot tea is meant to counteract the greasiness of some of the food. When you're ready for more tea, be sure to fill everyone else's cup before your own. When someone pours tea for you, say thank you by tapping the table with two fingers.

The original dim sum goes back to the Song dynasty (960–1279 CE) when travelers would stop in tea houses for small snacks. This tradition developed into dim sum as we know it today. Dim sum is mostly associated with Cantonese cuisine. Guangzhou, the capital of Guangdong, is a port city with lots of travelers passing through who'd stop in

tea houses for *yum cha*. *Yum cha* means "drink tea" in Cantonese, and it refers to having tea with two small dishes of food and to the concept of dim sum. Dim sum means "touching the heart."

The point of dim sum is to order lots of small dishes so you can try all kinds of different foods.

Rice is so closely associated with Chinese cuisine that many people assume the Chinese have it with every meal. But you can safely skip the rice when having dim sum. Dim sum is a big meal, and there are so many other options to try. You'll need to pace yourself so that you don't fill up too quickly. Besides, you can have rice any time.

When you go out for dim sum, the first thing you want to do is order tea. Tea is crucial for dim sum. It's a tradition that began in tea houses, after all. Then you can either order from a special dim sum menu—this will often have chef's special dishes on it—or order straight off the carts as they go by. Go ahead and order anything that looks tasty, and don't be afraid to try something new. The point of dim sum is to have small portions so you can try lots of dishes.

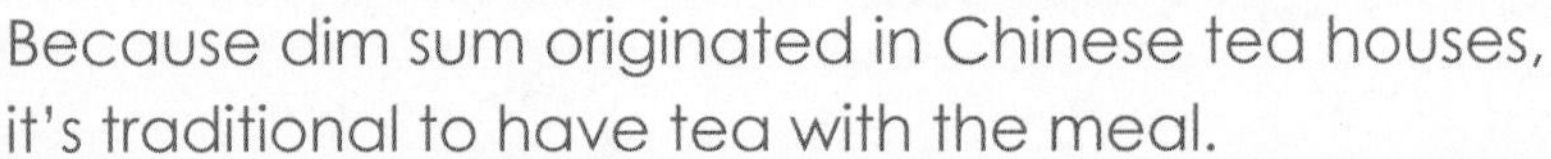

Because dim sum originated in Chinese tea houses, it's traditional to have tea with the meal.

Peking Duck

Of all the Chinese foods in the world, Peking duck may be the most spectacular. Eating Peking duck is a ritual. The reddish-brown roasted duck is often carved tableside by an experienced chef—the best can break the duck down into more than 120 pieces—into slices of juicy meat and crispy skin. It's served with typical side dishes of thin pancakes, green onion, shallot, special sauce, cucumber, garlic paste, and sugar. Peking duck is known as "the first dish to taste in China."

In China and in Chinatowns around the world, you'll see Chinese BBQ restaurants with rows of glistening, crispy roasted duck, chicken, and pork hanging in the windows. These restaurants slice and serve the meat over rice or noodles for a quick takeout lunch or dinner. Chinese chefs have perfected the art of cooking and storing meat this way.

"Peking" is an older word for Beijing. And

it's a little surprising that Peking duck is such a famous food of Beijing. Beijing is a city in northern China where pork, chicken, and lamb dishes are most common. Most traditional Chinese duck dishes come from places where there's more water. This makes Peking duck a luxury, and it was served frequently in the imperial court during the Ming dynasty (1368–1644).

Experienced chefs are able to slice Peking duck into more than 120 pieces.

The Chinese cleaver is one of the most versatile knives. Chinese chefs use a cleaver for almost all their food prep.

While chefs from Europe, Japan, and the United States have a whole arsenal of knives they use for cooking, Chinese chefs get most of the job done with just one knife: the cleaver, or *choy dao*. Chinese cleavers are small and more versatile than French cleavers, which are large and heavy so they can cut through bones. Chinese cooks, on the other hand, use cleavers for all kinds of prep work with vegetables and meat.

Some of the most famous restaurants to have Peking duck in Beijing are also the oldest. Bianyifang was established in 1416 and Quanjude was established in 1864. Quanjude is famous for using the hanging method to roast the ducks. After the skin is separated from the meat by pumping in air, the ducks are hung over the flames in the oven, giving them super crispy skin.

While it's still possible to get traditional Peking duck in Beijing, chefs all around the world are creating their own versions of this classic dish today.

Hot Pot

Hot pot isn't just a food. It's an event. A hot pot dinner should be had in a group and can last for hours. Hot pot, which comes from the Chinese *huoguo* ("fire pot"), is a pot of simmering broth placed in the center of the table with raw meats, seafood, vegetables, noodles, and condiments. Diners cook the ingredients in the broth throughout the meal.

Hot pot has existed in China for over 1,000 years. One of the most authentic places to have hot pot is Chongqing. Chongqing hot pot is known for its spicy red broth of super-hot chilis, Sichuan peppercorns, and beef **tallow**, which helps to mellow the spice of the broth. For dipping ingredients, just about anything goes: poultry, beef, seafood, vegetables. But some of the more interesting

> Hot pot is not the kind of meal you have alone on a Tuesday night. It's all about sharing. So hot pot should be enjoyed communally. Be sure to serve others as you serve yourself. But because it's a shared food experience, you want to avoid double dipping.

ingredients for non-Chinese eaters are **tripe** and duck intestines. The traditional way to cook tripe and intestines is the "seven ups and eight downs" method of repeatedly dipping the food into the pot to cook it while keeping it tender.

Hot pot is a great meal to serve for a party.

Glossary

caramelize To cook sugars until they develop a rich, brown color.

cereal food A grass that is cultivated for its edible seeds.

coagulate To become thickened into a single mass.

cuisine The style of cooking of a particular culture.

cultivation Raising plants for food in a controlled manner.

ferment To preserve a food or liquid by allowing yeast to convert the sugars in it.

garnish A decoration for food.

gelatinous Having a jellylike consistency.

glaze To put a sweet or savory coating of thick liquid on food during cooking.

marinate To soak meat in a flavorful liquid to tenderize it and add flavor.

mother sauce One of the five sauces that are the foundation of French cuisine.

savory Salty or spicy, usually opposed to sweet.

staple food The dominant food of a population's diet.

tallow A rendered form of beef fat.

tripe The edible lining of an animal's stomach.

umami One of the five taste sensations (along with sweet, sour, bitter, and salty) that has the rich flavor of fermented foods.

For More Information

The best way to learn about food is by tasting as much of it as possible. If you're able to, try as many different restaurants as you can. But you don't have to be rich to try lots of foods. Some of the most exciting food in the world is street food. And some of the best comes from the recipes of family and friends. Food blogs and recipe websites are also great resources. And a trip to the grocery store or a specialty market can be like a trip to a museum for foodies. Remember, food involves all the human senses. And because it's such an important part of human culture, it's all around us: look, touch, smell, listen, and most importantly, taste and enjoy.

Bibliography

Bramen, Lisa. "The History of Chopsticks." *Smithsonian Magazine*. August 5, 2009. https://www.smithsonianmag.com/arts-culture/the-history-of-chopsticks-64935342/.

Brickman, Sophie. "The History of the Ramen Noodle." *New Yorker*. May 21, 2014. https://www.newyorker.com/culture/culture-desk/the-history-of-the-ramen-noodle.

Carolyn, Phillips. "Get to Know Char Siu Ribs, AKA Pork Candy." *Bon Appetit*. September 22, 2016. https://www.bonappetit.com/restaurants-travel/article/chinese-char-siu-ribs.

China Daily. "Tofu Culture in China." February 12, 2011. https://www.chinadaily.com.cn/life/2011-02/12/content_11996892.htm.

Confucius Was a Foodie. "The History of Noodles." Accessed September 9, 2020. https://confuciuswasafoodie.com/noodle-timeline/.

Dunlop, Fuchsia. "Peking Duck: The Complex History of a Chinese Classic." *National Geographic*. July 9, 2021. https://www.nationalgeographic.co.uk/travel/2021/07/peking-duck-the-complex-history-of-a-chinese-classic.

Dunlop, Fuchsia. "The Rise (and Potential Fall) of Soy Sauce." *Saveur*. September 20, 2016. https://www.saveur.com/chinese-soy-sauce-history/.

Eating China. "Soy Story: The History of the Soybean." Accessed September 9, 2021. https://www.eatingchina.com/articles/soystory.htm.

Ejji Ramen. "You Won't Believe Where Steamed Buns Came From." May 31, 2017. https://ejjiramen.com/history-steamed-buns/.

Francis, Ali. "What Is Oyster Sauce? And How Do You Cook with It?" *Bon Appetit*. August 30, 2021. https://www.bonappetit.com/story/oyster-sauce-explainer.

Fulton, April. "Chinese New Year: Dumplings, Rice Cakes and Long Life." NPR. February 8, 2013. https://www.npr.org/sections/thesalt/2013/02/08/171455463/chinese-new-year-dumplings-rice-cakes-and-beyond.

George, Sarah. "7 Facts About Dim Sum for the Curious Foodie." ALLWOMENSTALK. Accessed September 9, 2021. https://food.allwomenstalk.com/food-facts-about-dim-sum-for-the-curious-foodie/.

Griffen, Peter. "Chinese Cleaver." Cook's Info. October 26, 2020. https://www.cooksinfo.com/chinese-cleaver.

Gu, Hallie. "China's Purchases of U.S. Soybeans Soared 53% in 2020, But Fell Short of Deal Target." *Star Tribune*. January 23, 2021. https://www.startribune.com/china-s-purchases-of-u-s-soybeans-soared-53-in-2020-but-fell-short-of-deal-target/600014368/.

Ho, Soleil. "Everything You Need to Know to Master Hot Pot." Thrillist. February 11, 2021. https://www.thrillist.com/eat/nation/what-is-hot-pot.

Huang, Kimi. "Peking Duck: History, Recipe, and How to Eat It." China Highlights. September 2, 2021. https://www.chinahighlights.com/beijing/food/beijing-duck.htm.

ifood.tv. "Chinese Rice." Accessed September 9, 2021. https://ifood.tv/chinese/chinese-fried-rice/about.

International Rice Research Institute. "China and IRRI." Accessed September 9, 2021. https://www.irri.org/where-we-work/countries/china.

Jampol, Sarah. "The Spice Blend That's Great on Ribs (and Also in Cookies)." *Bon Appetit*. August 20, 2019. https://www.bonappetit.com/story/what-is-five-spice.

Mulyanto, Randy. "Taipei's Tasty 'House of Stink.'" BBC. May 7, 2019. https://www.bbc.com/travel/article/20190507-taipeis-tasty-house-of-stink.

Ngo, Hope. "These Are the Secrets of Chinese Brown Sauce." The List. October 14, 2020. https://www.thelist.com/261345/these-are-the-secrets-of-chinese-brown-sauce/.

Omondi, Sharon. "What Is Terrace Farming?" WorldAtlas. September 17, 2020. https://www.worldatlas.com/articles/what-is-terrace-farming.html.

Ozimek, Sarah. "Hoisin Sauce." Curious Cuisiniere. April 22, 2021. https://www.curiouscuisiniere.com/hoisin-sauce/.

Ramen Culture. "China Origin." Accessed September 9, 2021. https://www.ramen-culture.com/history-pt1.

Ryerson, Lia. "You're Eating It Wrong: Noodle Etiquette Across the Globe." One Green Planet. Accessed September 9, 2021. https://www.onegreenplanet.org/vegan-food/noodle-etiquette-across-globe/.

Shingler, Tom. "Take a Bao: The Steamed Buns of China." Great British Chefs. November 9, 2018. https://www.greatbritishchefs.com/features/bao-steamed-buns-history.

Sterling, Justine. "The Many Origin Stories of Chop Suey." *Food & Wine*. May 23, 2017. https://www.foodandwine.com/news/many-origin-stories-chop-suey.

Travel China Guide. "China Geography." April 14, 2021. https://www.travelchinaguide.com/intro/geography/.

UNESCO. "The Great Wall." Accessed September 9, 2021. https://whc.unesco.org/en/list/438/.

Wan, Liv. "What Is Sesame Oil?" The Spruce Eats. July 22, 2021. https://www.thespruceeats.com/sesame-oils-in-chinese-cooking-4056391.

Waxman, Olivia. "Go Behind the Scenes as Fortune Cookie History Gets Made." *Time*. January 27, 2017. https://time.com/4645242/chinese-lunar-new-year-rooster-2017-chief-fortune-writer-wonton-food-cookie-factory/.

Wei, Clarrissa. "The Highs and Lows of China's Fried Rice Capital." Vice. April 28, 2017. https://www.vice.com/en/article/ypx3mg/the-highs-and-lows-of-chinas-fried-rice-capital.

The Woks of Life. "Mapo Tofu." September 7, 2021. https://thewoksoflife.com/ma-po-tofu-real-deal/.

The Woks of Life. "Rice Vinegar." November 29, 2019. https://thewoksoflife.com/rice-vinegar/.

The Woks of Life. "Soup Dumplings (Xiaolongbao)." August 17, 2020. https://thewoksoflife.com/steamed-shanghai-soup-dumplings-xiaolongbao/.

The Woks of Life. "Soy Sauce: Everything You Need to Know." December 28, 2020. https://thewoksoflife.com/soy-sauce/.

Zhang, Megan. "Sichuan Peppercorn: A Chinese Spice So Hot It Cools." BBC. November 11, 2020. https://www.bbc.com/travel/article/20201110-sichuan-peppercorn-a-chinese-spice-so-hot-it-cools.

Zhang, Na, and Guansheng Ma. "Noodles, Traditionally and Today." *Journal of Ethnic Foods*, Vol. 3, Issue 3. 2016. https://www.sciencedirect.com/science/article/pii/S2352618116300828.

Zhang, Sarah. "Rice Was First Grown at Least 9,400 Years Ago." *The Atlantic*. May 29, 2017. https://www.theatlantic.com/science/archive/2017/05/rice-domestication/528288/.

Index